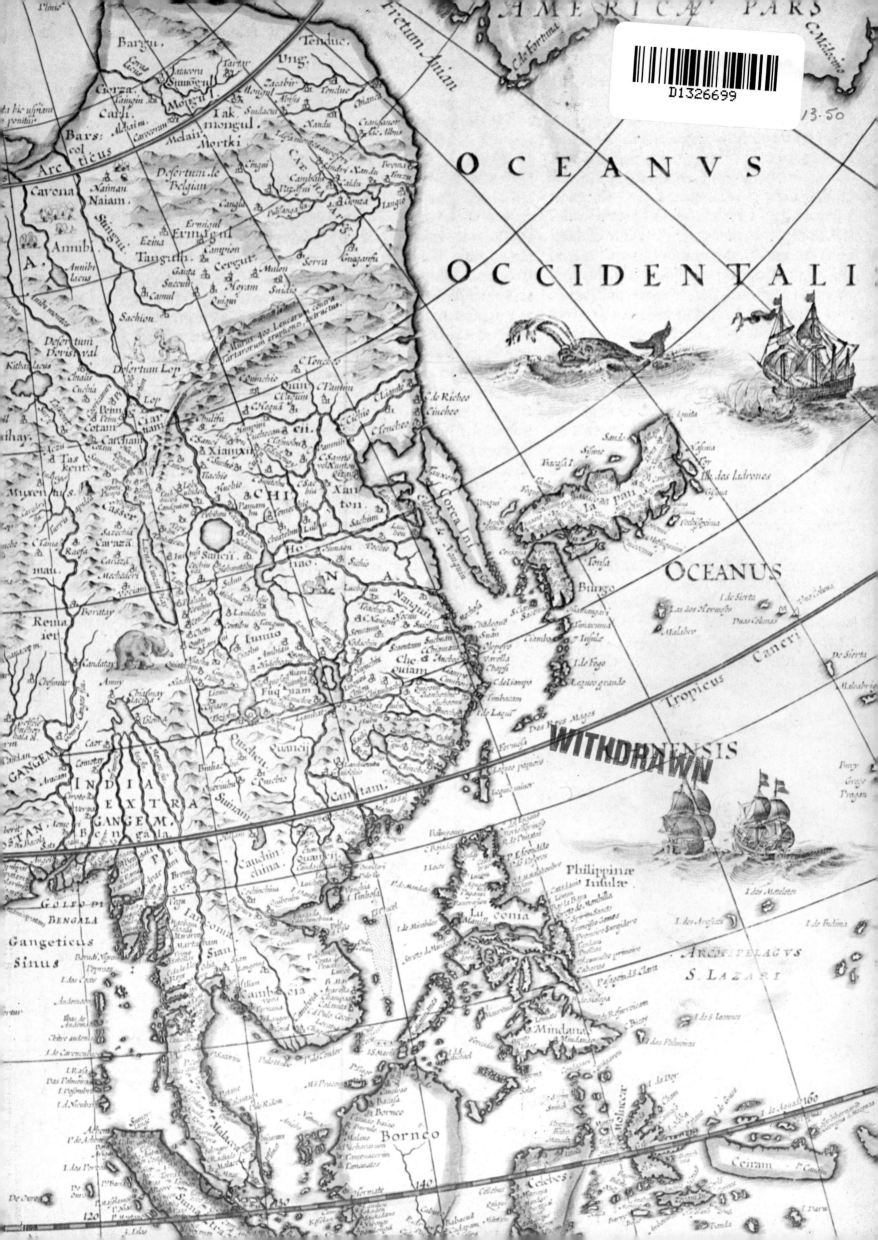

TEXT AND DIRECTION BY
Richard Z. Chesnoff

PHOTOGRAPHY BY
Larry Secrist with Jeffrey Aas

Philippines

PREFACE BY
Ferdinand E. Marcos
President of the Republic of the Philippines

INTRODUCTION TO MANILA BY
Imelda Romualdez Marcos
First Lady of the Philippines and Governor of Metropolitan Manila

Harry N. Abrams, Inc., Publishers, New York

(*endpaper*) Asia Noviter Delineata
Engraving by Guiljelmo Blaeuw, Amsterdam, 1638

(*this page*) Sampaguita, the national flower

Editor: Patricia Egan
Designer: Dirk Luykx

Concise Edition 1980

Library of Congress Cataloging in Publication Data
Chesnoff, Richard Z. 1937–
   Philippines.
   1. Philippine Islands—Description and travel—
1975–   I. Secrist, Larry. II. Title.
DS660.C47 1980   915.99′0446   80-18860
ISBN 0-8109-1475-1

Library of Congress Catalog Card Number: 80-18860

© 1978, 1980 Harry N. Abrams, Inc.

Printed and bound in Japan

Contents

Bay of Bongao, Tawi-Tawi
(preceding page)

Portrait of President Ferdinand E. Marcos, by Vicente Manansala. Oil on canvas, 1966. Collection Malacañang Palace, Manila

Preface

The Philippines comes to the modern world with a history distinguished for a variety of influences and cultural currents. The Filipinos were an ancient people, already in the process of constructing a state when Spanish sailors in search of a trade route landed on a Visayan island; long ago they established values and traditions that remain undiminished to this day, retaining the primeval scent of native soil, the marrow of old character and vision. While this ancient political and social system was evolving method and self-awareness, two colonial governments were superimposed on it, first in the sixteenth century and again as the twentieth century opened. Both colonizers inspired or imposed change, not infrequently causing protest and pain among the colonized. But the land and people have preserved and developed an essence all their own, a character and perception evocative of the light and weather that enveloped the stout sea craft of ancient *barangays* sailing in quest of new moorings in one or another of the archipelago's seven thousand islands. Through these islands at the same time voyaged ancient mariners bearing arms and implements of trade as well as set notions from everywhere—Chinese and Arabs, Malays and Indians, British and Dutch, Spaniards and Americans. Upon the land alien forces and elements converged, sometimes benignly, other times ruthlessly, to enter the indigenous culture, to blend passion and wisdom, routine and inventiveness, music and hubbub. Today still a crossroads, the Philippines is a country at once old and new.

This book of photographs captures this essence.

Richard Chesnoff and his crew of photographers caught this Filipino substance after traveling the length and breadth of the land, often taking side trips to out-of-the-way places, to corners that even natives may not have dreamed or dared to visit. The journalist and his crew were searching for something more than just the obvious, were in fact in quest, as I see it, of a special grail, the soul of the land and the spirit of the people. It was a big job. If I were a photographer I would pursue the same aim with equal single-mindedness, though the labor might seem forbidding.

The Philippines was caught unawares by photographer and writer as they strived to record and perpetuate it in light and shade, in the colors of life. I believe that they had a joyous and fulfilling time of it as they snapped their cameras and composed their reactions, for the Philippines is a rich land, not only in natural resources but in the diversity of its people. Sometimes one feels that one may point a camera anywhere in this country and achieve something rewarding for both the eye and the mind. Chesnoff and his crew chose their targets wisely and well. Before they clicked the shutter, they had sketched with the curious and naked eye the drama of a landscape or of a living face, the sap and substance of some human encounter on a city street, the permanence and power of an edifice, the order or chaos in a crowd of people, a stretch of countryside, a nuance of the country's history.

I am very happy about this, for the Philippines must still be explained to other people in other parts of the world.

This book, then, will make it easier for the people of other countries to experience an immediate discovery of the home of the Filipino people. The pictures tell many things about Filipinos and their birthplace. Having seen these pictures, one who has not set foot on the land, or who has seen it too quickly or only cursorily, will undoubtedly experience the thrill of a sudden intimacy with the people and their environment and startle himself with the thought: "I know this place and this people."

When this happens, I hope the impression will last for a lifetime.

". . . land of the sun caressed,

Pearl of the Orient seas, our Eden lost! . . ."

—"Last Farewell," José Rizal, 1896

Before there was the land, there was nothing but sea and sky and a great bird that flew in the sky. By and by the bird grew tired of its endless flight and began to search for a place to rest its wings. When it found none, it provoked a war between the sea and the sky. The raging sea hurled a tempest of great waves at the sky. The sky threw down a rain of giant boulders and gem stones. The boulders became the great continents. The gem stones became the islands of the Philippines.

Eventually, lush forests of bamboo grew up on the islands. The great bird returned and, landing on the tallest bamboo tree, began to peck it open. From it emerged Malakas, *the strong one, and* Maganda, *the beautiful one. These were the first Filipinos.*

—Tagalog legend

The actual origin of the land is almost as romantic as the legends that surround it. For, according to geologists, the Philippines was not born an archipelago of thousands of islands, but was once an integral part of the great continental shelf of the Asian mainland itself. It was a broad, green land of rich volcanic soil shadowed by towering mountains—some so tall that they dwarfed what we now know as the Himalayas. Then came the last Ice Age. And when it ended, less than ten thousand years ago, the land at the rim of the mainland began to sink. Finally only a group of the tallest peaks stood above the swirling waves of the China Sea. These are the Philippines.

Yet another geohistoric theory claims that the Philippines (together with Borneo, Java, Sumatra, the Moluccas, the Marianas, the Carolines, Guam, Hawaii, and other Pacific islands) are all that remain of a vast, lost continent. This Pacific Atlantis, say the theoreticians, was destroyed in prehistory by a series of massive eruptions and earthquakes.

Whatever the case, the land that remains above the waters is a land forever linked to the sea—by geography, by history, and by culture: an archipelagic nation of more than 7,100 tropical islands, some so small that they virtually disappear from sight at high tide, others so great that it can take days to traverse them. Only 462 islands are more than one square mile in area, and barely 1,000 boast of any population. All told, the land area of the archipelago equals 115,830 square miles, and the entire chain of islands stretches 1,150 miles in length. This is the northernmost region of the East Indies; it is an integral part of Southeast Asia, with Borneo barely thirty miles from the country's southernmost tip and Taiwan sixty-five from its northernmost isle. A few miles west of Taiwan lies the Asian mainland itself.

Geographers usually divide the Philippines into three island groups: Luzon in the north is the largest; the Visayas, in the middle, is a scattering of medium-size islands; Mindanao to the far south is also

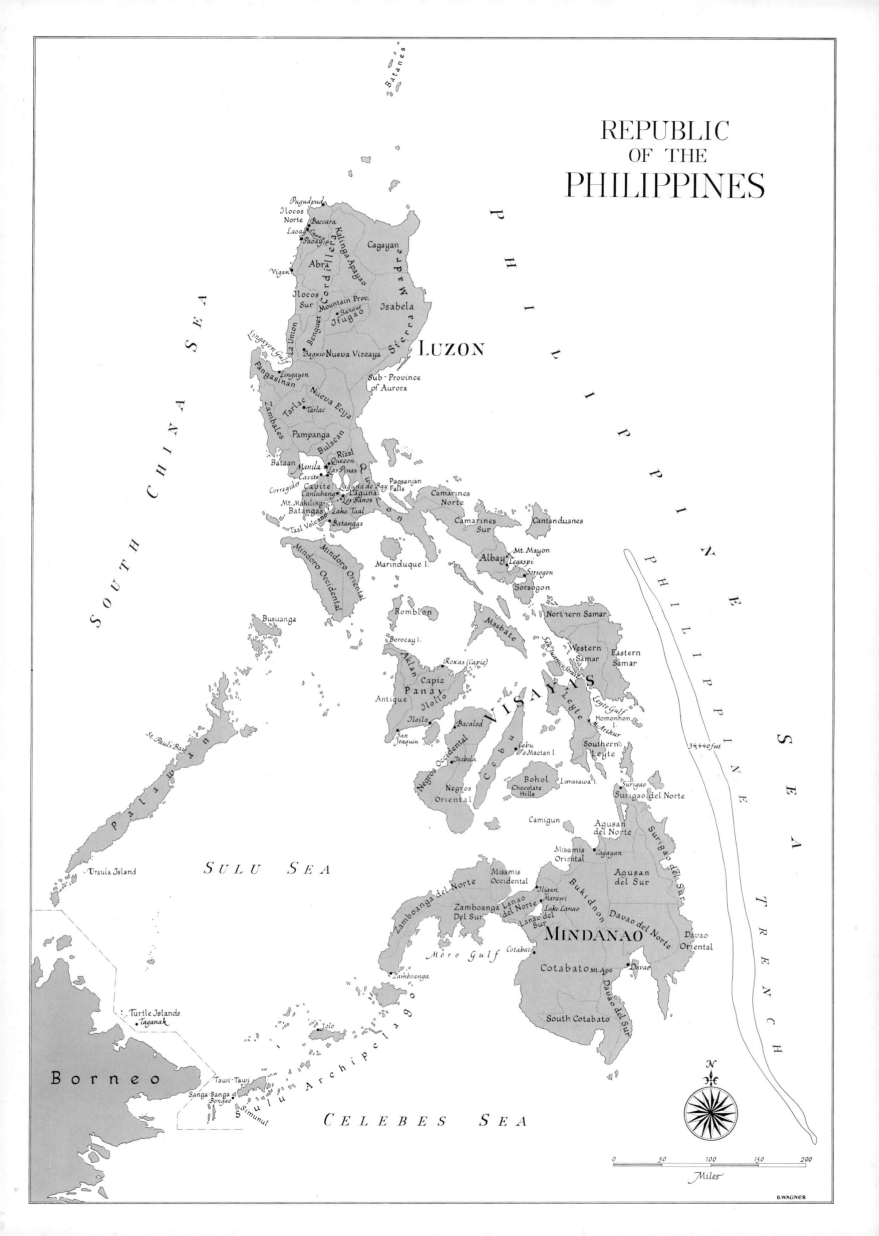

vast—and a world and culture apart. The waters that wash the sandy shores of the Philippines—the Pacific Ocean and the China, Sulu, and Celebes seas—and the proximity of the equator have blessed the islands with a lush tropical climate. The result is a land of mist-covered peaks and great green plains, of lush rain forests, waterfalls, and rivers, of emerald gulfs and coral bays, all tied in an everlasting cycle of life to the great seas themselves. "Land and Water," writes author Carmen Guerrero Nakpil, "are the central facts of our lives."

The green of the islands is as staggeringly beautiful as it is varied—from tiny, spidery ferns to towering hardwood trees. Botanists estimate that there are at least 10,000 species of ferns and flowering plants. And while most Philippine plant life is tropical, species familiar to more temperate zones can be found high in the mountain regions.

There is little that can be compared with the beauty of the flowers. Their colors are rich, their perfumes deep—and they are everywhere. For the Philippines is a wonderland where flowers grow in wild abundance; trails of pink bougainvillaea, white and crimson daisies, red hibiscus, orange straw flowers, the gentle but heady white sampaguita (the national flower), and the crowning glory of orchids—at least 900 varieties of these alone. Some, like the cattleya, are giant and queenly; others, such as the smaller waling-waling, grow in great speckled sprays.

The forests where many of the orchids hide cover more than half the land area of the Philippines and, together with vast stores of minerals, represent much of the country's prime natural resources. They are also home for Philippine fauna: 700 rainbow varieties of butterflies and at least 739 species of birds, from fierce monkey-eating eagles that rule the crests of mountains to courtly white cockatoos, raucous green plumed parrots, and tiny black rice birds. There are pythons and caymans, lemurs, deer, squirrels, wild boar, and the ubiquitous carabao—the water buffalo that is partner to every Filipino farmer. Although the Philippines may not boast of any of the majestic beasts that roam continental Asia, it possesses unique zoological wonders. Three mammals are peculiar to the Philippines: the gargoyle-like tarsius, the smallest of all monkeys, found on the island of Bohol; the tiny mouse-deer of Palawan; and the nearly extinct tamaraw, a wild carabao that roams the heights of the Mindoro mountains.

Of all living treasures, however, none are in greater abundance that those of the sea. More than 2,000 varities of fish—among them grouper, halibut, tuna, and marlin—fill the oceans with a bounty that many believe will provide for the ultimate future of the nation.

Today, more than forty-four million Filipinos enjoy the fruits of these seas and fertile shores. Their story is one of centuries of immigration and of the melding of the personality of a sea people—a fusion of Malay-Polynesian stock with Chinese, Indian, European, and American blood and culture. This multiplicity of roots and multifaceted cultural heritage has given the Philippines its unique role in Asia and in the world.

There are signs that a primitive form of man may have roamed the region of the Philippines 250,000 years ago. But the pioneers who settled the islands probably wandered across the land bridges during Paleolithic times. Doubtless some were ancestors of the Aetas, or Atis, the curious Negrito tribes whose modern descendants are still found in isolated pockets on Luzon and Mindoro. Others were likely proto-Malay in racial type. The remains of some of these first Filipinos have been discovered at the Tabon Caves on Palawan, dated by archeologists and anthropologists at 20,000 B.C. Tiny in size, these cave dwellers lived by hunting but they also gathered wild fruits and practiced a primitive form of agriculture.

When the ice melted and the land bridges disappeared beneath the waves, other more culturally advanced tribes began to cross the seas from the Asian mainland. Tall, lean, and light-skinned, they were members of an early Stone Age group which anthropologists classify as "Indonesian A." A second wave of straight-haired, darker-skinned immigrants arrived about 1500 B.C. from Indochina and southern China. Classified as "Indonesian B," they landed on Luzon, engaged in dry agriculture, and built villages of houses with pyramid-shaped roofs. And between 800 and 500 B.C. another wave of sea-borne settlers arrived from Indochina, bringing with them copper, bronze, and a knowledge of irrigation and rice culture that would eventually become the root base of all Filipino agriculture. The foundations of a people had been laid.

These first Filipinos were the forebears of the country's indigenous tribes: the Kalinga, Igorot, and Apayaos of Luzon; the Tagbanuas of Palawan; the Bagobos and Manobos of Mindanao; and the other minority groups whose unique tribal cultures survive to this day in isolated mountain and jungle villages.

But the foundations of modern Philippine culture and society were laid only later, with the massive waves of Malay immigration that began in 300 B.C. and continued into the fifteenth century A.D. Intrepid sailors, these brown-skinned, brightly garbed Malays crossed uncharted seas in great sailboats, bringing with them tools and weapons and the arts of pottery and weaving. They introduced the horse and the carabao, they cultivated the fields and grew fruit trees. They had a written alphabet. Their government included *datu* chieftains, and a communal system called the *barangay* which is still the basic Philippine political unit. By the beginning of the Christian era the Malays had gained preeminence over the islands. And in the Philippine melting pot it is the Malay personality that remains at the core of the national sensibility.

The seafaring Malays attracted trade and traders—and in the process, contact with the other great civilizations of the East. Each of these left a mark upon the Philippines. Arab traders en route to China brought with them the culture of India. Hindu concepts of divinity soon became incorporated into local religious beliefs; Sanskrit words and characters crept into the local dialects; Indian motifs were adopted in crafts and in fabrics. To this day the *barong tagalog,* the pineapple-fabric shirt worn by Filipino men, is similar in cut and design to the *kurta* of Southern India.

The same Arab traders took word of the Philippines on to Canton. And the Chinese soon began to send their own ships and cargoes to the nearby islands. Delicate Chinese porcelain dating from the sixth century A.D. has been uncovered in archeological digs, evidence that there was early contact. Trade with Canton grew, and by the time of the eleventh-century Sung Dynasty permanent Chinese settlements had been established in the archipelago, bringing another lasting influence to bear on the cultural and racial personality of the Philippine people.

As Islam spread throughout the Malay Peninsula, it brought still another influence. Arab missionaries laid the groundwork and built mosques in Tawi-Tawi as early as the fourteenth century. By the fifteenth century, warlords from Sumatra had established sultanates on Sulu, Jolo, and on Mindanao; by the sixteenth century, entire Mindanao tribes had embraced the faith of Muhammad, and even parts of Luzon were in Muslim hands.

Islam might well have conquered all of the islands had there not arrived, one morning in 1521, three galleons in the service of the Spanish crown. Ferdinand Magellan and his small fleet had been at sea for almost two years before they sighted the green shores of the isle of Samar. At first the Portuguese-born explorer and his half-starved men thought they had discovered the fabled Spice Islands. When they landed on the beach they flung themselves down in gratitude, raised the cross, signed a treaty in blood with a local tattooed chieftain, the datu Kolambu, and claimed the entire archipelago in the name of the king of Spain.

It was a momentous meeting between Occident and Orient. For 350 years Spain would dominate the Philippines, christianizing its people, adding to the racial and cultural mix, and finally leaving to it a sense of identification with Western culture that forms an ineradicable part of the Philippine consciousness, unmatched anywhere else in Asia.

Spain's conquest of the Philippines by sword and cross did not go easily. Magellan himself soon fell in the battle on Mactan at the hands of Lapu-Lapu, a Filipino warrior chieftain who was unenthralled with the idea of foreign colonizers. And although the Spaniards dubbed the islands *Filipinas* in honor of the prince who became King Philip II of Spain, it was not until half a century later, when they finally captured the native town of Manila and established their own capital there, that they gained a real foothold in the islands.

For most of Spain's three and a half centuries of Philippine ownership, Madrid governed Manila through Mexico (the Hispanic cultural influence in the Philippines is, in fact, largely Mexican). Great galleons constructed of Philippine mahogany plied the Pacific from Manila, carrying cargoes of silk, spices, gold, and tobacco; they returned from Acapulco laden with silver—and with soldiers, priests, and bureaucrats. For colonial rule was a cynical combination of evangelism and avarice. The *conquistadores* and the friars who came to govern the land were often as eager to exploit its wealth as they were to convert its "little brown people" into Christians.

The people whom the Spaniards came to convert already possessed their own distinctive religious, political, and cultural systems. Epic poems such as the Ilocano "Life of Lam-ang" were passed orally from generation to generation. Other poems and dramas were written on bark and on bamboo tubes. A religion of soul spirits was centered for the most part around a Supreme Being called "Bathala." And there was a political system that featured equal rights for women and a social ladder on which even a slave could rise to become a noble.

But the Filipinos suffered from an unfortunate central weakness: the absence of any sense of national unity. Instead, they were divided into countless tribes and dialects: the Ilocanos, Pampangueños, Tagalogs, and Bicolanos of Luzon; the Warays, Boholanos, Cebuanos, and Ilongos of the Visayas; and in Mindanao, at least a hundred other forms.

To maintain control over these peoples, the Spaniards sought to minimize any sense of national pride or of peoplehood. Filipinos were taught to think of their own culture and of themselves as inferior. The silks and brightly colored costumes of the Tagalogs, Visayans, and other Filipino peoples were discarded for affectations of European garb. The Latin alphabet replaced pre-Spanish syllabism and the population was urged to adopt Spanish surnames.

The Spanish language, on the other hand, was not taught to the majority of the natives. With ruthless logic the *conquistadores* argued that if one language replaced the babel of regional dialects, it might help the Filipinos to unite against colonial rule.

Notwithstanding, Spanish rule did not go unchallenged. The mountain tribes of Luzon and the Muslim tribes of Mindanao resisted Spanish attempts at conquest for almost four hundred years, and christianized lowlanders in Luzon and the Visayas made at least three hundred sporadic revolts. By the end of the nineteenth century, open yearnings for Philippine national expression had developed and could no longer be suppressed, especially among the western-educated generation of young Filipinos knows as *ilustrados*—the enlightened ones. Their strongest voice belonged to Dr. José Rizal, whose first novel, *Noli Me Tangere,* published in 1886, exposed both the graces and misdeeds of Spanish colonial rule. A gifted physician and artist as well as writer, Rizal had studied and worked in Europe. He returned home to the Philippines to seek reforms, rather than independence from Spain, but even this was considered too dangerous by the Spanish colonial regime. The Spaniards exiled Rizal to Mindanao; then, on December 30, 1896, he was executed by a firing squad at Fort Santiago in Manila.

But the sun was already setting on the Spaniards in the Philippines. Formed by Andres Bonifacio in 1892, a secret nationalist society called the *Katipunan* preached Filipino unity as well as open revolt. And the Katipunan soon gave way to a revolutionary army led by General Emilio Aguinaldo that waged fierce guerrilla war against the Spaniards and inflicted heavy losses upon them. This was the period, says historian Teodoro Agoncillo, "when the natives became Filipinos."

But foreign forces came again into play. Spain and America had gone to war over Cuba, and in May, 1898, Commodore George Dewey defeated the Spanish fleet in Manila Bay. The Americans struck an alliance with Aguinaldo and his rebels, and while the Revolutionary Army continued to defeat the Spaniards on land, the Americans blockaded them by sea. Spanish rule in the Philippines was effectively ended.

Aguinaldo and his Revolutionary Army decided to grasp their chance for freedom, and on June 12, 1898, in Kawit, a quiet town in Cavite, south of Manila, Aguinaldo declared an independent Philippine nation. It was the first republic to be proclaimed in Asia, and the revolution that had brought it about was the first successful uprising against colonial rule in the Orient. But the young republic was short-lived. By virtue of the Treaty of Paris, late in 1898, and over the objections of Aguinaldo and his revolutionaries, Spain "ceded" the Philippines to the United States for twenty million dollars. Outraged, the Filipinos took up arms again to fight against their erstwhile American allies. Finally, after four years, the remnants of Aguinaldo's army surrendered. The Philippines had a new foreign master.

The Americans, like the Spaniards, couched their colonial rule in altruistic slogans, but United States presence brought colonial rule with a difference. Public education was introduced, and it helped to make the Philippines into the third largest English-speaking country in the world today as well as one of the most literate. The Americans built roads and hospitals; they boosted the economy—albeit geared primarily to their own export-import needs—and raised the standard of living. Above all, they provided the basis for a modern democratic state and promised eventual self-government. A constitution was adopted and a commonwealth established in 1935 with Manuel L. Quezon as its first president; independence was scheduled for 1945.

World War II and the vicious Japanese invasion early in 1942 interrupted the march of the Philippines toward freedom. Despite a heroic stand, the Filipino-American defending forces were overwhelmed by the invaders. For nearly three years the people of the Philippines suffered a brutal Japanese occupation, then the horrors of a devastating war of liberation. When it was all over in 1945, hundreds of thousands had died, and *barrios,* towns, and even the capital city of Manila had been all but leveled. On July 4, 1946, against this background of still-smoldering ruins, the Republic of the Philippines at last became free of foreign rule and achieved full independence.

The next quarter century saw the young republic struggle under the weight of staggering problems. A succession of presidents—Manuel Roxas, Elpidio Quirino, Ramon Magsaysay, Carlos P. Garcia, and Diosdado Macapagal—tried to solve these, each in his own way. But the legacy of centuries of colonial rule and disunity—partisan politics, corruption, and total control of the economy by the wealthy—crippled progress. Reforms remained slogans and the gap between haves and have-nots increased. Rebellion was growing in the countryside and near-anarchy in the city.

Faced with this the country's sixth president, Ferdinand E. Marcos, elected in 1965 and reelected in 1969, placed the Philippines under martial law in 1972 and launched a revolutionary program to establish a new political system in the Philippines, geared to what he saw as the needs and realities of the country's people. The people of the Philippines, said President Marcos, would build "a new society of equals."

Marcos' experiments with constitutional authoritarianism were not without critics who accused him of having shattered the Philippines' western-style democracy. But some of his harshest critics soon had to admit that the "New Society" had opened the Philippines to a wave of change. Indeed, the economic and social progress it brought about in its first few years surpassed all the accomplishments of the preceding generation.

Above all there was a recognition of roots and a new sense of nationhood, much of this evident in a vivid new flourishing of national arts: in the music of José Maceda and Lucrecia Kasilag, in the dance theater of Alice Reyes, in the writings of Nick Joaquin and Cirilo Bautista, in the paintings and sculptures of Arturo Luz and Hernando Ocampo, and in the inventive new work of a host of young artists; in everything, from new designs for the national costume—the *barong* shirt of the men and the butterfly-shouldered terno dress of the women—to the flowering of Pilipino, the national language based on the Tagalog dialect.

The Philippines also began to assume leadership in its own region of Southeast Asia as well as in the rest of the developing world. At the same time, it expanded friendly ties with nations of East and West. This westernized nation with its roots deep in the East continued to play its historic and its geographic role as a cultural bridge between Orient and Occident.

Indeed this multiplicity of understanding, this capacity for adaptability, lies at the core of the Philippine national personality. Thousands of years of contact with other cultures and peoples and of the intermingling of bloods and beliefs has produced a unique people, possessed of a liberal approach to their own life and to that of others. For the Filipinos themselves—*barrio* farmer, fisherman, and urban dweller alike—are ultimately a people of many parts. The Malay in them gives them their openness to change; the Chinese, their sense of dignity and inscrutability; the Spaniard, their love of drama and fiesta; the American, their frankness and their drive to move forward. Like the many parts of their island nation, the Filipinos and the distinct Filipino culture that is emerging from this marvelous mixture make a synthesis of it all, a total people.

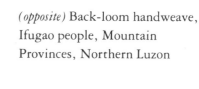

Northern Luzon

From the harsh hills of Ilocos and the tall forests of Cagayan down through the green plains of Tarlac and Pampanga stretches Northern Luzon—the broadest landmass on the Philippines' largest island. Like the rest of the nation, it is a tapestry of varied landscapes and cultures. To the far northwest lies Ilocandia, hemmed in on one side by the China Sea, on the other by the Cordillera Mountains. The *conquistadores* came here in search of gold, bringing with them a rich Hispanic culture that is still very much part of the countryside. They found a rugged land that was transformed by a rugged people into an agricultural heartland.

To this day the people of Ilocos are considered the epitome of industry and frugality. And the hundreds of thousands of Ilocanos who have migrated to other parts of the Philippines and throughout the world beyond have carried this hardy spirit with them.

Hardy too are the Igorot people, the tribal groups whose colorful villages perch atop the pinewood-forested peaks of Luzon's Mountains Provinces. Never conquered or colonized, the Igorots have carved their farms and monumental rice terraces by hand out of the mountainsides.

The southern stretches of the Mountain Provinces are rich with minerals—gold, silver, and copper. The lowlands to the west are lined with the white sand beaches of La Union and Pangasinan and the bountiful waters of the China Sea. To the east, beyond the Sierra Madre, lie the Pacific Ocean and the equally rich waters off the coast of Isabela and Quezon. Here, for these people as for a majority of Filipinos, the sea, with its more than 2,000 species of fish, provides food and livelihood.

Still, rice is the mainstay of the Philippine diet. And the great central plains of Nueva Ecija, Tarlac, and Pampanga, and the Tagalog provinces to the south, are the rice bowl of the Philippines, with hundreds of thousands of acres under rice cultivation.

From the first rains in May to the harvests the following March, millions of Luzano farmers painstakingly tend their paddies in an endless life-giving cycle.

A Batanes Island farm woman in a raincape of coconut leaves and husks enjoys a home-grown cigar *(above)*.

The fields of Ilocos produce most of the garlic used in the Philippine cuisine *(left)*.

In Ilocos Norte, on the northern tip of Luzon, dawn breaks over the Cordillera Mountains *(following pages)*.

A carefully kept window garden *(above)* and an old-fashioned *calesa* rig *(right)* are a few of the many reminders of Laoag's long, proud past. Already a major town in pre-Hispanic times, Laoag was settled more than a thousand years ago by the Malays who built villages alongside the *locos*—coves— that dot the coast of the China Sea and gave the Ilocos region its name.

Rugged and for the most part isolated from the rest of the country, Ilocos was frequently attacked by pirate fleets. Laoag's few welcome visitors in ancient times were the traders from Japan and China who came to sell porcelain and fabric, and the highland tribesmen from the east who sailed down the Laoag River to barter gold, venison, beeswax, and other mountain products in the market square.

In 1572 an expedition of Spanish explorers led by Juan de Salcedo sailed from Manila to explore Ilocos, and after encountering resistance, finally managed to occupy Laoag. Nevertheless, it remained a center of anticolonial rebellion in the centuries that followed; the Ilocos region itself has been a wellspring of rugged men and women.

A

B

E

A sense of beauty, color, and design is evident in the Ilocano arti-facts as well as in the objects of daily use: A) detail of silver altar frontal; B), D), G) details of designs from the rear of *calesa* carriages; C), H) market baskets; J) straw hats; I) palm-leaf packaged cheese; E) detail of wall, Paoay church; F) bolts of Ilocano homespun cloth.

The great church at Paoay with its pinnacles and scrolled buttresses (*following page*) is a unique combination of Gothic, Baroque, and Oriental designs. Built of coral blocks and stucco-plastered brick, its facade and outer walls are decorated with relief designs made of a local mixture of sand, lime, sugarcane juice, and egg yolk. Begun in 1704 and finally completed in 1894, it remains a monument not to the Augustinian friars who ordered its construction, but to the Paoayeño peasants who designed and built it.

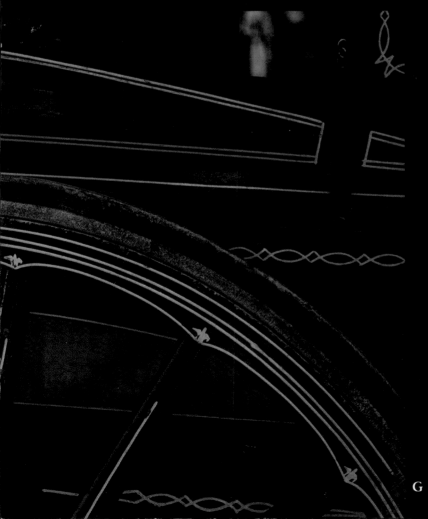

G   H

C

D

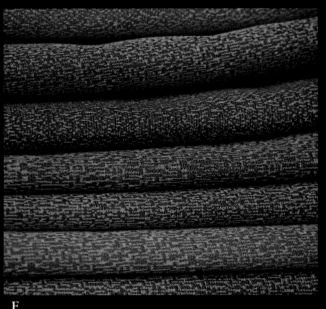

F

I J

Like a giant stairway to the gods, the rice terraces of the Ifugao people stretch up thousands of feet toward the cool blue skies in the Mountain Provinces. No one knows when these engineering marvels originated, but the highland tribesmen who carved them by hand from mud and stone are believed to have begun them over two thousand years ago. Many of the terraces already rise to an altitude of 5,000 feet, completely encircling entire mountains; their makers' descendants still continue the work, adding level after level to the ledge paddies and to the ingeniously intricate irrigation system that has linked them from year to year, century after century. It is the world's oldest ongoing construction project, and, like the rings of a tree, the awesome rice terraces trace the history of a proud mountain people's battle for survival.

The terraces at Banaue *(left, and following pages)* are the most famous in the Philippines for their magnitude as well as for their accessibility to outsiders. Emerald green in the planting and growing months of December through May and purple-yellow in the harvest months of June and July, the Banaue terraces cover an area of 400 square miles. Placed end to end they would stretch ten times the length of the Great Wall of China.

Banaue is also the homeland city of the Ifugao, among the fiercest of the warrior-farmers who live in the Cordillera region. Thought to have immigrated by land bridge from the highlands of Burma thousands of years ago, the Ifugao resisted all attempts at outside domination. They are wood craftsmen and weavers, as well as farmers; they cling to their polytheistic faith and to the independence that was theirs long before Western foreigners first marveled at the sight of Banaue.

At Mayaoyao, on a plateau in the Cordilleras, the neat pyramid-shaped homes of the Ifugao villagers are reflected in the waters of ledgelike rice paddies *(preceding pages)*.

In the hills surrounding Baguio is also the campus of the Philippine Military Academy *(above)*.

Scented pine forests and flower gardens ring the cool mountain city of Baguio (*following pages*). A popular resort in the hot "summer" months of February, March, and April, Baguio was the first American-built city in the Philippines. Its stately homes include the presidential palace at Mansion House.

Lingayen Gulf off the coast of Pangasinan, west of the Mountain Provinces, is dotted with scores of tiny lime-stone islets *(above and following pages)*. Known as the Hundred Islands, they are a land- and sea-garden of flowers and fish.

INTRODUCTION TO

Manila

We Filipinos call **Manila** "the city of our affections." This historical phrase is taken from old Spanish writings, but it also expresses a quite modern sentiment.

Manila is all things to all Filipinos. It is the seat of government, the fashion center, the intellectual pace-setter, the fountainhead of all religious and educational movements, and, of course, one enormous shopping arcade. It is politics and art, markets and churches, banks and universities—the whole of life.

For most Filipinos—especially those who have yet to visit Manila—it is the political and economic summit, the city of dreams. For the millions eking out a living in its slums and for its westernized middle classes caught in traffic jams, it is an asphalt jungle—gaudy and ruthless but irresistible.

Manila's most winning characteristic is its unflappability. It is an old city, older than historians can determine; perhaps having been around for a long time gives it its poise.

Manila was a Malay settlement trading with Chinese and Annamese junks when its documented history began, sometime in the twelfth century. In 1565, when the Spanish *conquistador* Miguel Lopez de Legazpi arrived at Cebu in the Philippine archipelago, he was told by boastful natives that he must see their large city further north on the island of Luzon. He took their advice and sent two fleets to conquer it. The first flotilla reported back its defeat at the hands of the Malay chieftain Rajah Sulayman, who defended with cannon, sword, bamboo lances, and stout-hearted men his palisaded city built where the Pasig River flows into the great bay. The next year, 1571, Sulayman burnt his city and retreated to the orchards along Manila Bay, the site of today's tourist belt.

The first Spanish documents recount that the ancient Manilans were charming people, exquisitely clean—for they took two or three baths a day—fond of colorful cloths and addicted to jewelry and merriment, extremely pleasant and generous to a fault. On the whole, those qualities remain with us to this day.

Manila has led a far from placid existence. After Legazpi's conquest it was assaulted by a succession of Chinese warlords, Dutch and Portuguese fleets, and a British occupation force. It was occupied by the Japanese in 1942 and retaken—and in the process leveled to the ground—by the U.S. forces in 1945.

The history of Manila is the history of the Philippines. For 200 years it was from Manila that the galleons carried Chinese silk to the New World. It was from inside Intramuros, the old walled city of Manila *(following pages),* that Spanish governors-general and archbishops ruled the archipelago for 330 years. From

Manila's slums the secret revolutionary society, the Katipunan, recruited its members. It was in old Fort Santiago that the Spaniards executed our national hero, José Rizal, and in San Juan, a hamlet a few miles north of its center, Filipinos fought the first skirmish of the Philippine Revolution against Spain in 1896, and the first battle of the Philippine-American war of 1898. It was in Manila that Philippine independence was finally recognized. And in Manila flourish the finest and oldest universities, the art galleries, the Philippine Cultural Center, and a new complex of convention centers and tourist hotels.

But it is not only historical vicissitudes that Manila has endured. There were also those of the elements. Manila lies almost two feet below sea level, in the path of vicious typhoons and earthquakes. Despite the best efforts of the Metro Manila Commission, and the cooperation of its more than eight million citizens, Manila is beset by seasonal floods, by a summer which often reaches almost 100 degrees in the shade, and by occasional earthquakes.

But what are a few battles and cyclones for a city and a people who have always survived? Unlike many an old capital city, Manila is not jaded or dispirited. And unlike many a modern, congested city, it is not cynical, its people are not depersonalized. Even if I say so myself, Manila and its people have the grace, strength, and wisdom of the past and the joy, love, and optimism of the future. It is truly a city of man.

Imelda R. Marcos

Ships have come to call and anchor in Manila Bay for more than a thousand years. In the distance, the port of Manila; in the foreground, the boat basin on Roxas Boulevard *(opposite page)*.

Two of the most visible landmarks of modern Manila: the popular "Love Bus" transport system *(left)*, and the Metro Manila Aides *(below)*, the snappily uniformed army of street cleaners that keeps the city clean twenty-four hours a day.

The Cultural Center of the Philippines is Manila's showcase for the arts and artists—Filipino as well as foreign *(preceding pages)*. A project of the First Lady, Imelda Romualdez Marcos, the CCP was designed by Leandro V. Locsin and constructed in 1969 on land reclaimed from the sea. Its vast concert hall and theater are capped by an arts library, galleries, museums, and facilities for music and art workshops. Adjoining is the International Convention Center, Trade Center, Folk Arts Theater *(right and below)*, and the Philippine Plaza Hotel *(left)*.

Every January tens of thousands of worshipers flock to the Quiapo church in downtown Manila to venerate a lifesize gold-adorned image of the Black Nazarene *(following pages)*.

The multipassenger jeepney, or minibus, which began as a utilitarian postwar transport system, is now ubiquitous in the urban scene—and a unique mobile museum of Filipino folk art (*preceding page*).

Manila's *Nayong Pilipino*, or Philippine Village, is a living national museum in which are assembled plants, wildlife, lifesize replicas, and original artifacts, from houses to handicrafts, coming from every region of the Philippines. The "village" has its own rice terraces, sugar fields, orchid farm, and even a model of a volcano. Seen above are a re-creation of a mosque and a Maranao chieftain's house in Mindanao.

The early nineteenth-century bamboo organ in the church of San José at Las Piñas is a unique blend of Malay and European instrumental arts. The organ is twelve feet wide and has 174 bamboo pipes (*right*).

Malacañang Palace on the banks of the Pasig River is the official residence of the Philippine president.
Originally built in the eighteenth century as a Spanish aristocrat's country estate, it was given its name by
the Tagalog fishermen who used to sail past it: *"May lakan diyan,"* they would say—"Nobles live in that place."

At the American Cemetery in Manila simple white marble headstones mark the graves of more than 17,000 soldiers—Filipino and American—who fell in the World War II battle to defend the Pacific.

Across Manila Bay the sun sets over Bataan and Corregidor, "The Rock," the last bastions to fall to the Japanese in 1942 *(following pages)*.

Although weakened by hunger and severely outnumbered by the Japanese, the Filipino-American garrison at Corregidor held out during twenty-seven days of shelling so severe that it changed the topography of the island. The ruins of Mile Long barracks and rusting cannon emplacements stand as monuments to their heroism (*left*).

The 310-foot cross on the peak of nearby Mount Samat commemorates the courage of the troops who died in the battle for Bataan and on the infamous Death March that followed its fall (*above*).

Phalaenopsis amabilis, a *mariposa* or moth orchid native to Mount Makiling *(right)*.

Southern Luzon

South of Manila, the island of Luzon twists and turns like a great green serpent. At the serpent's head, within sight of the city itself, is Laguna de Bay, the largest inland body of water in the Philippines. By day the vast lake's 355 square miles of blue water are alive with the spidery armed *salambaw* rafts and bamboo traps of the fishermen who live by its shores. By night the waters sparkle with the glow of thousands of filament lamps hanging from the booms of fishing boats.

The fertile farm landscape of Laguna Province is a series of gentle plains and quiescent volcanoes. The most famous of these is the 3,575-foot Mount Makiling, whose peak is said to be haunted by the spirit of a nymphlike goddess named Mariang Makiling.

Laguna is also the home and birthplace of the most famous Filipino, the national hero, Dr. José Rizal, whose writings and leadership at the turn of the century gave birth to the revolutionary movement that eventually won the Philippines its independence.

Neighboring Cavite Province also boasts a famed native son, General Emilio Aguinaldo, who declared Philippine independence there in 1898 and became the infant republic's first president.

Like Laguna, Cavite is still largely agricultural. But both provinces have a wide agro-industrial base and an expanding industrial foundation. Lush Batangas Province to the south was formed largely of lava from the province's once-formidable Taal Volcano. In addition to being an agricultural paradise, Batangas is considered one of the Philippines' finest cattle-ranching regions.

Southeast of Batangas, coconut-ringed coastlines curve along Quezon and on through to the Bicol provinces of Camarines Norte (among the country's richest mining regions), Camarines Sur, Albay, and down to Sorsogon and the southern tip of Luzon. At Albay, the near-perfect cone-shaped volcano of Mount Mayon rises from sea-level plains to almost 8,000 feet. Often totally veiled in mist, still-active Mount Mayon towers over nearby Legaspi City and the rich lava fields of the region—a constant reminder that the province and its people are eternally linked to the fury as well as the wealth of the great volcano.

The fields of Canlubang *(right)*, lying at the foot of Mount Makiling, are among the finest sugarcane fields and farmlands of Laguna.

Taal Volcano is in fact the most furious of the Philippines' eleven active volcanoes. More than thirty spectacular eruptions have been recorded since 1572, some so devastating that rains of fire, mud, and smoke all but destroyed the region and its population. Yet, unlike Mount Mayon, Mount Apo, and other volcanoes whose majestic cones dominate the landscape around them, Taal is a mere 984 feet high, barely rising above the shoreline of the lake.

Lake Taal itself actually fills what remains of the crater of another immense, now-extinct volcano. This prehistoric Taal Volcano may have been as high as 18,000 feet, and on its slopes lay the entire area of what is now Batangas Province, receiving its lush soil from the ashes, mud, and lava of centuries of volcanic eruption *(following pages)*. At some point before recorded time the cone of this monster volcano collapsed, leaving a great depression in its wake. Sweet water rushed in to fill the void, forming a crater lake seventeen miles long, twelve miles wide, and so deep that it has never been fathomed.

Only the tip of the original volcano remains above the waters. The lava and basaltic rock that poured forth over the centuries eventually created a twelve-square-mile island within Lake Taal itself. New fissures and craters appeared, and nestled within one of these is another lake, greenish yellow in color *(pages 72–73)*, with yet another small volcanic cone in its center. Thus this island is in a lake on an island in a lake on yet another island—Luzon.

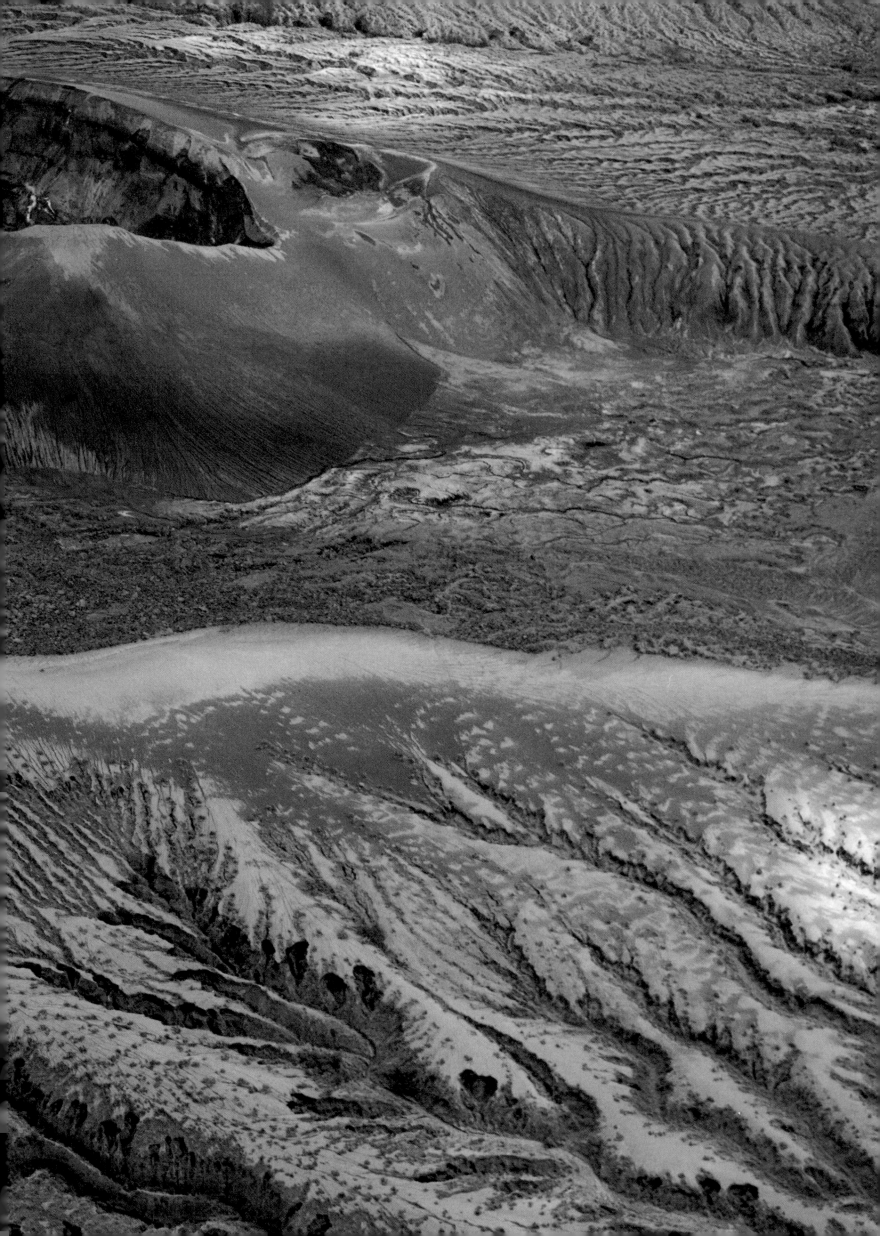

The wild green mountain-island of Mindoro, south of Luzon, is rich in minerals and ringed with coral and sand beaches (*left*).

On nearby Marinduque Island, Holy Week culminates in a passion play devoted to the story of St. Longinus, the Roman centurion who helped to crucify Jesus but thereby became a convert to Christianity. The male population dons costumes that have grotesque handcarved masks as their major feature (*following pages*).

The slopes of Mount Mayon dominate the province of Albay at the southern tip of Luzon (*pages 78–79*). Considered the world's most perfectly shaped volcanic cone, Mount Mayon rises 7,946 feet above sea level and is believed to be at least 10,000 years old. Its first recorded eruption took place in 1616 and there have since been fifty fiery torrents. The worst of these occurred in 1814, when rock, lava, and volcanic ash from Mount Mayon completely buried Cagsawa, leaving only a church tower as a reminder of what once was a town.

(*right*) Canna, Bandera española

Visayas

The emerald islands of Visayas are the "Old South" of the Philippines, a tropical paradise where the fruit falls from the trees and the fish all but jump into the net. It is a warm place of easy living and casual temper, of smiling women and elegantly simple houses of bamboo and palm; a land where song and dance are a language as much as is the dialect of each island.

The two eastern islands, Samar and Leyte, are especially rich in farms, forests, and fish. Separated only by the swift waters of the San Juanico Strait, the two are linked in history. It was Homonhon Island, off the south coast of Samar, that Ferdinand Magellan first sighted after crossing the Pacific in 1521. And two weeks later on Limasawa Island, south of Leyte, the Spanish explorer signed a blood oath with the chieftain Kolambu and then celebrated the Philippine Islands' first Catholic mass. More than four centuries later, when the United States forces landed at Leyte in 1944, the Visayan waters would be the scene of the fiercest naval battle in human history.

Like Leyte and the rest of the lush Visayas, the island of Bohol is a major producer of copra, the dried coconut meat from which oil is expressed. The western rim of the island is set with a strange, almost symmetrical array of haycock-shaped "Chocolate Hills" that change color with the seasons—from green to dark brown.

The port of Cebu City on the nearby finger-shaped island of Cebu is the Philippines' second largest city and a major shipping depot for copra, sugar, logs, and fish, and for mangoes, grapes, and other fruits of the Visayan belt. Cebu City too has shared in Philippine history, for on nearby Mactan Island Magellan died in battle with the island chieftain Lapu-Lapu.

Negros and Panay islands are the sugarbowl, two sprawling islands to the east whose lowland plains stand tall with sugarcane in fields that stretch as far as the eye can see. And although the life and economy here have begun to change, both the countryside and the major cities of the islands—Bacolod and Iloilo—have distinctive charm. The grand *haciendas* and Antillean-style mansions of yesterday's sugar barons, the Spanish Baroque churches and the decidedly gentle pace—all speak very much of the past.

The Marcos Bridge, 7,026 feet long, spans the San Juanico Strait between the island provinces of Samar and Leyte (*left*). Part of the Philippine-Japan Friendship Highway that will link the entire archipelago, it is also a popular subject for local artisans who weave with abaca, the raw material used for Manila hemp (*above, below*).

We came to Leyte just before midnight of a dark and moonless night . . . and waited for dawn before entering Leyte Gulf. . . .
About 50 yards from shore, we waded in . . . . When it was done, and I stood on the sand . . . ready to talk into the microphone,
the rains came down. This is what I said: "People of the Philippines: I have returned."

—*General Douglas MacArthur,* Reminiscences, *New York, 1964*

The massive landing of 200,000 United States and Filipino troops on Leyte's Red Beach on October 20, 1944, launched the liberation of the Philippines from the Japanese and marked the beginning of the end of a terrible war *(left)*.

Centuries of living with typhoons, tidal waves, and earthquakes have taught Filipinos to build homes that are easily replaced. And in the *barrios* of Leyte, the building materials of palm leaf and bamboo are right at hand. Here, as throughout the country, no house is considered complete without its own green garden *(above)*.

The island of Bohol, near Leyte, was one of the first explored by the Spanish, who were intrigued by the more than a thousand oval-shaped limestone hills that dot the island's central plain *(following pages)*. Covered with cogon grass that makes them as green as giant gumdrops during the rainy season, the strange mounds turn chocolate brown in the dry months—thus earning their name, the Chocolate Hills. According to legend, they are the hardened teardrops of a giant whose love was spurned by a beautiful island maiden.

Large quantities of ancient Chinese porcelain and other artifacts have been uncovered on Cebu, archeological evidence of the trade that thrived between the Philippines and Canton as far back as the sixth century. There was a large, permanent community of Chinese merchants and traders on the island long before the Spaniards arrived, and Cebu's Chinese community is still one of the largest in the Philippines *(above)*. The Chinese community also chose the city as the site on which to build the great Taoist Temple, a multileveled complex of bright-colored pagodas, dragons, and lions.

The port of Cebu was the site of the first major Spanish colonial settlement in the Philippines and today it is the country's second largest city. Its most revered possession: the Santo Niño de Cebu, a richly robed, handcarved wooden image of the infant Jesus, said to have been a baptismal gift presented by Magellan to the converted wife of Humabon, the chieftain of Cebu, in 1521 *(left)*.

The Santo Niño played a major role in the Spanish conversion of the Philippines to Catholicism; although the Filipinos were largely unimpressed by the image of the crucified Christ, they were fascinated with the concept of an infant King Jesus. Today nearly every church in the Philippines has a Señor Santo Niño of its own.

Magellan died on the shores of nearby Mactan Island *(following pages)*, attacked by the fierce local chieftain Lapu-Lapu.

Nipa, bamboo, and rattan provide the raw materials for everything in a *barrio* on Panay, from the house to the handwoven mat for drying the rice crop *(above)*.

Sugar is king in the Visayas and more than sixty percent of the country's entire crop is grown on the islands of Negros and Panay, where it is processed into mountains of raw sweetness, then shipped abroad. Sugar fortunes helped to build the city of Iloilo on Panay in the eighteenth and nineteenth centuries, and the classic Antillean-style houses that line many of its gardened streets help to retain its air of antiquity *(right)*.

During the three-day carnival-like fiesta of Ati-atihan on Panay Island, local citizens make merry in elaborate costumes, their skin blackened with soot in imitation of the aborigines who once ruled the islands *(above)*.

A water buffalo finds wet solace in a flowery pond *(right)*.

The delicate form of a bamboo fish trap is outlined against a Visayan sunset. Fishing is a prime industry in the Visayas—as throughout the Philippines—and it is rapidly replacing sugar as the base of the region's economy.

Mindanao

Mindanao is the future. Vast, and with some areas still uncharted, it is an island of fertile plateaus and mineral-rich mountains, mighty waterfalls and towering rain forests. It is also blessed with a climate free from the typhoons that rage across most of the Philippines. The result is a promised land of enormous economic potential.

The wealth of the Philippines' second largest island is spread across its length and width. To the northeast, the emerald and sapphire seas reach inky depths of more than 35,000 feet, the world's second deepest ocean trench. Surigao, Bukidnon, and Agusan provinces, rising from the northern coastline, have rich timberland as well as deposits of nickel, copper, silver, and gold. Further west and south, in Davao and Cotabato, are the broad green fields of Asia's largest banana, pineapple, and abaca plantations. Furthest west lies the Zamboanga Peninsula; here the Sulu Sea yields pearls and coral as well as hundreds of varieties of fish.

Because it has always attracted immigration, Mindanao's culture is an especially exotic patchwork. In prehistory the first Filipinos wandered here, across the land bridges that once linked the island to Borneo. Thirteen of these aboriginal tribes still live in inland villages scattered across the mountains and jungles. Some, like the Higaonon, T'boli, and Blit, have highly developed cultures of their own with textiles of intricate weave and jewels of rainbow colors. Others, like the gentle Tasaday of the Cotabato rain forests, remain only a step away from the Stone Age.

Muslim tribes represent the largest minority in Mindanao and account for about ten percent of the island population. The stilt houses and many-colored *vinta* boats of the seafaring Moros line the southern coast. The white-domed mosques and intricately carved *torogan* houses of the proud Maranao people guard the shores that surround the azure waters of Lake Lanao.

The promise of Mindanao has also attracted millions of Christian settlers from throughout the archipelago.

This mighty convergence of cultures has caused certain conflicts, and at times bitter warfare has raged between Christian and Muslim Filipinos—much of it fanned by outsiders. Off the breakwater of Zamboanga City the hope for the future is symbolized by a huge white tower decorated with both cross and crescent.

The mighty 300-foot Maria Cristina Falls in Iligan, in northern Mindanao (*left*), has been harnessed to generate much of the electric power used in the south. Like the lush rain forests of the island, the falls are among Mindanao's richest resources.

The fiercely proud Maranaos were the last of the Mindanao peoples to convert to Islam, and they are among the most observant of all Muslim groups in the Philippines. At least one minaret and domed mosque rises in each of their lakeside villages (*following pages*).

Mount Apo, the tallest mountain in the Philippines, stands almost 10,000 high. Its peak, once the mouth of a fiery volcano, now rises quietly among the clouds *(left)*. Several hundred feet below the peak lies a green plateau surrounded by lush forest and flowers *(above and below)*.

In Rio Hondo, on the edge of Zamboanga Peninsula, the day begins with the muezzin's call. The fishermen who live in this exotic sea village of bamboo catwalks and houses on stilts are descendants of the Tausogs, Samals, and Badjaos—the seafaring Muslim tribes that sailed the Moro Gulf *(above)*.

Mindanao men go down to the sea in ships—in large fishing trawlers as well as in the multicolored *vinta* sailboats (*following pages*) that are a favorite of Moro seamen.

Palawan and the
Sulu Archipelago

Palawan and the 1,769 small coral islands that speckle the seas around it comprise an archipelago within an archipelago. Long and narrow (364 miles by 5.27 miles, at its narrowest point), it stretches like a dagger to the southwest, almost touching the shores of Borneo. This is rugged country. Along the western coast a chain of mountain ranges has peaks that rise to more than 6,000 feet; giant birds nest in the caverns and niches of its heights. To the east the natural harbors and bays that line the shore are made all but unusable by the shoals and coral reefs that guard the coastline.

Yet much of Palawan's land is fertile. Streams and rivers (including a subterranean river flowing into Saint Paul Bay) criss-cross the major island. The rolling countryside of the island of Busuanga, in the north, has been developed into cattle ranchland. Of even broader potential importance are the major oil deposits that are known to lie beneath the stormy seas of Palawan's western shores.

The Sulu archipelago, south of Zamboanga and parallel to Palawan, falls like so many stepping stones to Borneo. In ancient times this was still a land-track to Indonesia, and even now one can see at night the twinkling lights of Bornean towns from some of the southernmost islands.

This is a world apart from the rest of the Philippines. The 2,600 volcanic and coral islands that comprise southwestern Sulu are scattered across the Celebes and Sulu seas like green dots on the broad blue ocean, some totally isolated from the others. It was to these islands that Arab missionaries came in the fourteenth century, bringing with them the faith of Islam that would later spread northward to Mindanao and even Luzon. Once ruled by Muslim sultans, it is an island country of seafaring peoples—of fierce Tausog tribesmen, of the pearl-diving Samals, and of the gentle Badjao sea gypsies whose entire lives are spent aboard tiny handcarved wooden craft that wander from one palm-fringed island to another.

Because so much of it is still wilderness, Palawan is rich in wildlife, some unique to the island. The tiny mouse-deer, or *Pilandok*, found nowhere else in the world, is the smallest known species of hoofed mammal (*below*). Palawan's bird life is also prolific and includes a unique species of peacock as well as several species of highland eagle, among them the rare Monkey-Eating Eagle (*left*). The Tamaraw, a tiny but fierce wild buffalo, is found only on Mindoro Island, north of Palawan (*above*).

Ursula Island sits like an emerald in the blue sea off the coast of Palawan
(left). Part of a national Philippine network of game refuges and bird
sanctuaries, the tiny (seven and one-half acres) coral island is home for tens of
thousands of wild doves who take flight each morning before dawn to forage
for food on the other islands of the archipelago, then return at dusk *(above)*.
During certain times of the year great flocks of migrating multicolored birds
also come to roost in the orchid-filled trees of Ursula Island. Brightly colored
fish dart in and out of the coral forests that surround its shores *(below)*.

Throughout the year the sea scatters shells and pieces of coral along the
island's white beaches *(following pages)*.

The island of Jolo is home for thousands of Tausog fishermen and their families *(above and right)*, many of whom live in a classic Tausog city on stilts.

A strange freshwater lake lies within yards of the rich coral coast of Jolo *(below)*.

Far south of Jolo lies the island group of Tawi-Tawi, the southernmost pearls in the Philippine string. Fishing villages dot the white sand beaches *(following pages)*.

(left to right) Photographers Jeffrey Aas
and Larry Secrist, and assistant Felix Blas

ABOUT THE PHOTOGRAPHERS

*Larry Secrist was born in Annamosa, Iowa, in 1942
and received his B.A. and M.A. degrees from the Brooks
Institute of Photography in Santa Barbara, California.
Secrist, whose works appear in galleries and museums
across the United States, makes his home along the rugged
Monterrey coast of California, which is the subject of
many of his unique photographic essays.*

*Jeffrey Aas, who comes from Albuquerque,
New Mexico, has worked under Mr. Secrist's tutelage
since 1971.*

PHOTOGRAPHING THE PHILIPPINES

Our photo schedule in the Philippines, as set for us by our director, Richard Chesnoff, was a formidable one.
Over a three-month period we were to photograph the land and its people—from Batanes in the far north to
Tawi-Tawi in the far south. Considering the vast coverage as well as the climatic conditions and time schedule
under which we would be working, my associate Jeffrey Aas and I selected the following equipment:

Large Format: (1) Linhof Teknika 4x5; (1) 150mm Schneider f/5.6; (1) 210mm Schneider Repro f/9;
(1) 300mm Schneider Repro f/9; (1) 90mm Schneider Super-Angulon f/8; (1) 65mm Schneider
Super-Angulon f/8.

Medium Format: (2) Hasselblad 500cM camera bodies; (1) 80mm Zeiss Planar f/2.8; (1) 150mm Zeiss
Sonnar f/4; (1) 250mm Zeiss Sonnar f/5.6; (1) 50mm Zeiss Distagon f/4; (1) Hasselblad Super-Wide
w/38mm Zeiss Biogon f/4.5.

Miniature Format: (2) Leica M-4 camera bodies; (1) 50mm Leitz Summicron f/2; (1) 135mm
Tele-Elmarit f/2.8; (1) 35mm Leitz Summicron f/2.8; (1) 21mm Schneider Super-Angulon f/3.4.

Conditions in a tropical climate present unique problems to successful color photography. High
temperatures and high relative humidity are the prime enemies of color photographic materials. We faced a
special challenge in using the completely new Kodak E-6 Professional Ektachrome film. This film was then
so new that it was virtually untested under the field conditions that we met. The new film must be refriger-
ated before and after exposure, and optimum results are claimed if it is processed within twenty-four hours.
For periods of up to two weeks we were far from such facilities, and this level of control was often beyond our
reach. However, the precautions that we took to protect our fresh and exposed films from the heat and
humidity proved adequate in most cases.

Because the E-6 process was not yet available in the Philippines, our film had to be shipped to San
Francisco every ten days or so to be processed there. We airshipped our exposed stock in a special canister
packed with dry ice. The special handling graciously afforded us on these occasions by the personnel of
Manila International Airport and the Philippine Airlines greatly contributed to the success of our venture.

We were also blessed in having the aid of our "grip" and chief assistant, Felix Blas of Laoag,
Ilocos Norte. Felix, whom we had met on our first location trip, remained with us throughout our entire
assignment, an indefatigable source of assistance, information, and good humor.

Larry Secrist
Carmel, California

ABOUT THE AUTHOR

Richard Z. Chesnoff has covered Western Europe, North Africa, and the Middle and Far East, reporting on many of the major stories and personalities of our times. Born in New York in 1937, Chesnoff became a correspondent for the New York Herald Tribune and NBC-News. In 1966, he joined the staff of Newsweek, where he served as a writer and correspondent, and eventually as Executive Editor of Newsweek International. Mr. Chesnoff divides his time between his travels and his home in Connecticut.

AFTERWORD

I first visited the Philippines in February, 1976, and was immediately enchanted. So when a Philippines book was first mooted with Andrew Stewart, President of Harry N. Abrams, Inc., it was clearly to be a labor of love. It was also a complex task, for the archipelago has more than 7,100 islands. That we succeeded was thanks to the incredible hospitality encountered everywhere.

It is impossible to name all who helped us, but I would like to express some special appreciation. I am deeply grateful to their excellencies President Ferdinand E. Marcos and the First Lady, Mme. Imelda Romualdez Marcos; they honored us not only by contributing their words to this volume, but also by showing so much personal enthusiasm. Without them, *Philippines* would have been impossible.

My deep appreciation also to Maj. Gen. Fidel V. Ramos, Col. Reynaldo San Gabriel, and the Philippine Constabulary; to Rear Adm. Ernesto Ogbinar of the Philippine Navy; to Maj. Gen. Samuel Sarmiento of the Philippine Air Force; and to the helicopter crews who made our aerial photography possible. The officials in each of scores of provinces, towns, and *barrios* went out of their way to help our project, as did a host of other Filipino friends. Foremost among them: Mr. and Mrs. Luis A. Yulo of Manila. Flight plans and film shipments were kindly coordinated by Philippine Airlines, and by Luis Tabuena, General Manager of Manila International Airport, and his super-efficient girl friday, "Pressy" Valdez. Many other public officials were helpful. I would like to thank especially Marita Manuel, J.C. Tuvera, the indefatigable Fe Gimenez, Ileana Maramag, and Vilma Bautista. Thanks, too, to Director Gregorio Cendana of the N.M.P.C., Minister of Tourism Jose Aspiras, and the staffs of the University of the Philippines, University of Santo Tomas, and the National Museum.

Special appreciation to Nai Chang, Dirk Luykx, and Patricia Egan of Harry N. Abrams, Inc., for their enthusiasm and enormous talent. There are not enough words to express my gratitude to my wife, Susan, who stood so closely by my side. Thanks also to my two stepsons, Ian and Paul Warburg, who shared our adventures, and to my son, Adam, who cheered us on from afar.

Finally, thanks to all the smiling people whose names I do not know: to the Tibi-Tibi tribesmen in Mindanao who built a nest of brush beneath our helicopter in hopes "the great bird would lay an egg"; to the old lady in Iloilo who let us photograph her treasured family *santos*; to the *barrio* farmer in Dingras who shared his lunch of fish and rice with us; to all the people of the Philippines, *salamat at mabuhay*! Thank you and long life! May this volume enable others to see you, understand you, and love you as we have learned to do.

Richard Z. Chesnoff
Manila, August 20, 1980

PHOTOGRAPHIC CREDITS

All photographs are by Larry Secrist, with Jeffrey Aas, except for those on the following specified pages: 43, 114, 115 (top), 126A, Dick Baldovino; 113, 117 (bottom), Hans Mueller; 76, 77, 124, 126C, 127C, Richard Z. Chesnoff; 127D, Juanito Acasio.

EVRO
PAE
PARS

ASIA
noviter delineata
Auctore
Guiljelmo Blaeuw.

NOVA
ZEMBLA

SAMO
IEDI

BAI

TAR

TAR

Ioughoria

Kaski Tartari

GRE
CIA

Morea

Severiens
is due

Cri
mea.

Pontus
Euxinus
sive Mare Magiore

Astracan
Nagai

Mare de
Sala vel Bachu
seu Chualensko more

CATAY

MARIS

MEDITERRANEI PARS

Candia

Cyprus

Famagusta

NATOLIA

AEGYP

Arden

ARABIA
DESERTA

Caldar d.
Caldea

PERSIA

FARSIA

ORIZ

Sigistan

Cabul

Candahar

Guza
rata

AFRI

SINAE

MARE RVBRVM

AYAMAN
olim

ARABIA
FELIX

Theama

Aden

Ormus

Sinus Persicus

Ormus

MARE

ARABICVM
et INDICVM

DE

CAE PARS

Zocotora

C. de Guardafui

OCEANVS

Aequator